Hounslow-Heath. A Poem

3| p.193

HOUNSLOW-HEATH.

BY THE REV. W. WILKES.

1748.

HOUNSLOW-HEATH.

A

P O E M.

The SECOND EDITION.
Carefully CORRECTED AND ENLARGED.

Venatu vigilant pueri, sylvasque fatigant
Flectere ludis equos, et spicula tendere cornu
Convectare juvatque prædas———
VIRG. Æn. 9.

——————— *En, age, segnes*
Rumpe moras ; vocat ingenti clamore Cithæron
Taygetique canes, domitrixque epidaurus equorum,
Et vox sensu nemorum ingeminata remugit.
VIRG. GEOR. 3.

By the Rev. Mr. WETENHALL WILKES, *M.A.*
Minister of the chapel at *Hounslow,* in the patronage of RICHARD BULSTRODE, Esq.

[*Privately re-printed, in aid of the funds collected for the restoration of Hounslow Church, by William Pinkerton, F.S.A., F A.S.L., who has added some notes on the locality.*]

ONLY ONE HUNDRED COPIES PRINTED.

LONDON:
JOHN CAMDEN HOTTEN, PICCADILLY.
1870.

INTRODUCTION.

AMONG my collections for illustrating the history of printing in the town of Belfast, I have a book entitled "*An Essay on the Existence of a God,*" by Wetenhall Wilkes, Sub. Gra., Belfast, 1730. And I was much surprised at meeting with the same man again, as "Minister of the Chapel at Hounslow," and author of the poem called "*Hounslow Heath,*" at the end of which he acknowledges the authorship of the *Essay.* The poem is of a very mediocre description, but I determined to privately reprint it, as a literary curiosity, forming a vehicle for some miscellaneous notes I have collected about the locality, and as my contribution towards the proposed restoration of Hounslow Church.

Of Wilkes I know almost nothing. There is a short "*Essay on the Resurrection*," at the end of the above-mentioned "*Essay on the Existence of a God*," and an introduction to it is dated Carrickfergus, 1729; probably he was curate there, but nothing is known of him in that locality now. From the letters Sub. Gra. after his name, I conclude that he was Under Graduate of some University, but in the lists of both Oxford and Cambridge his name is absent. In the Catalogue of Graduates of the University of Dublin, compiled by my late lamented friend, the Rev. J. H. Todd, D.D., Senior Fellow, the name of Wilkes is also absent; but the books of the junior graduates are unfortunately missing from March, 1717, to January, 1718, which must have been about

the time that Wilkes entered that University.
For there is no doubt that he entered it, and
I may presume that he was named after Edward Wetenhall, who, from 1678 to 1699, was
successively Bishop of Cork, Ardagh, and Kil-
more. He did not stay long at Hounslow, for I
see by the twentieth volume of the *Gentleman's
Magazine*, that he was preferred to the Rectory
of South Summer Court, in Lincolnshire, in
April, 1750, where he did not live a year,
having died, according to Musgrave's MS.
Obituary, on March 25th, 1751.

WILLIAM PINKERTON, F.S.A., F.A.S.L.

AN

EPISTLE

To His GRACE the

Duke of A - - - - LL,[a]

With the SECOND EDITION of

HOUNSLOW-HEATH.

Nec minus considerabo quod aures tuæ pati possint, quam quod
virtutibus debeatur. CIC. Orat.

DESCEND, Great Sir, accept my humble
  strains,
 And nobly grace my musical remains !
 Though to your taste sublimer lays belong,
With favour yet indulge my labour'd song.
Fain would the Muse make choice of your great
  name,
To be her patron, ornament, and theme.

Cherish'd by you, her tributary lays
In time would swell, and ripen into praise.
Her tuneful toils no trivial subject claims,
At no ignoble flight her purpose aims :
She sings not slaughter'd heaps——no horrid fights,
But rural sports, and innocent delights.

Soon as th' arrival of your Grace* was hear'd,
A rising gladness all our spirits cheer'd :
With heart and voice we Providence address,
To bless that life, which does so many bless.
The Muse attempts your safe approach to greet,
And lay this early homage at your feet.
Her just concern does in your absence shew,
Th' intense regard we to your presence owe.
For you she strikes the warbling lyre,——to you
Her honest songs of gratitude are due.

Thou God of Numbers, touch the warbling lyre,
And with thy rays my rural song inspire !
Sing A——ll's name, who does thy glories raise,
Whose name adorns and dignifies my lays !
Arm then, thou queen of verse, the task to try ;
Turn to th' inviting theme thy daring eye ;
Where goodness smiles, where loyalty is grac'd,
With sweetness, candour, and the finest taste ;

* At *London*, on the 5th of *Nov.*, 1748, from a long journey, and after several months absence.

With friendship, justice, and benevolence,
Extensive knowledge, and the soundest sense ;
With honour strict, sincerity of mind,
With love of industry,—with truth refin'd,
With unaffected air, with grace serene,
The patriot blazons throughout all his mein ;
In ev'ry scene well qualified to please,
To act at once with dignity and ease ;
A friend to liberty, and sacred right,
Albania's glory,——*Britain's* true delight.

Forgive, Great Sir, these truths,—but then to you,
All this applause, and more, is justly due.
With ev'ry social virtue thou art fir'd,
With ev'ry elegance of soul inspir'd.
In you transfus'd great *Campbell's* spirit reigns,
And unmix'd honour swells in all your veins.
Those rich, innate embellishments make good,
Th' hereditary worth of noble blood ;
That you was born o'er senates to preside,
To be your country's ornament and pride ;
To raise her dignities, defend her laws,
And crown yourself with well-deserv'd applause.

Possessing all the present age's fame,
The scholar's sanction, and the Muse's theme ;
With pow'r enrich'd, in health and balmy peace,
(Divine companions !) may your years increase ;

And may you stand possest of every grant,
That Heav'n can give, or mortal being want.

I am,

Your Grace's most dutiful,

And most obedient servant,

Wetenhall Wilkes.

Hounslow,
Nov. 14, 1748.

HOUNSLOW - HEATH,

A

POEM.

ET plodding cits, great sir, indulge their
    vein;
    And, ever anxious in pursuit of gain,
    'Midst smoke and noise drudge on in anxious
      care,
While in stagnation sleeps the lazy air.
Let giddy crowds in nightly revels sport,
And feast on all th' illusive joys at Court;
In museful solitude whilst I prepare,
An humble off'ring for the good and fair:
And you, great sir, from toil of State retir'd,
Deign to attend the song yourself inspir'd.

Assist, ye sacred Nine, the sports rehearse
Of *Hounslow Heath**—a word not seen in verse ;
Hounslow—unknown to all the tuneful throng,
A place ne'er mention'd in descriptive song ;
Presumes to vie, though not in equal strains,
Or with the *Roman*, or *Thessalian* plains.
Pure is the air, the prospects unconfin'd ;
And various are the sports t' unbend the mind.
Shall ancient *Hounslow* then be lost to fame,
And dull oblivion desecrate the name ?
No—from the Nine we this advice receive,
That in their records, *Hounslow's* name shall live.

Hail happy scene, secure from factious noise,
From pomp, from cares, from all delusive joys ;
From all expensive, criminal intrigues,
From levee, court, and drawing-room fatigues ;
Where sloping glades extend their length'ning lines,
Where Nature drest in gay disorder shines ;
Where spacious valleys part the mighty mounds,
And heathy shrubs o'erspread the tufted grounds ;
Where verdant lawns fill up the space between,
And beauteous seats adorn th' extensive green ;
Where soaring larks awake the dewy plains,
And tempt the Muse to sing the rural scenes ;
Where wilds present a wide extended view,
Far as the circling eyesight can pursue.

* *Hounslow Heath*, in the county of *Middlesex*, 4293 acres
and upwards, 1 Stat. 37 *H*. 8, 2.

The sports *Rome* boasted here may be renew'd,
And every *Roman* exercise pursued.

Four large patrician (*b*) elms behind the town
(True as a beacon to the trav'ler known)
Their lofty boughs with ancient pride display,
And to fair *Whitton* point the cheerful way,
Calliope first strikes the vocal shell,
To sing those scenes, where peace and grandeur dwell.
Whitton demands her verse——the *Nine* conspire,
To swell my numbers with poetic fire.
There Nature's genial pow'rs impregn the ground,
And all her fragrant sweets are spread around.
(Sweetest of birds!) there *Philomela* charms
The list'ning shade, and midnight hour alarms.
There should my wonder dwell, and there my praise,
Should soar sublime, and flow with tuneful ease.

A——*ll* to native elegance of mind,
Has contemplation and experience join'd ;
Unblemish'd honour, tenderness of heart ;
Candour, and wisdom, well improv'd by art ;
A firm, unshaken, uncorrupted zeal,
Not vainly blazing for his country's weal ;
But steady, bold, and regularly free,
For *Britain's* glory, and for liberty.
Nor is he skill'd in awful schemes alone,
To serve his king, and to defend the throne.

His bosom, which pure principles refine,
Still labours glorious with some great design.
With Truth exalted, all his words display,
Unstudied humour, ever kind and gay.

O fit to shine in Courts—to rule the State,
Or to appear in soft retirement—great!
Thy patriot virtues, and exalted mind,
With goodness in sweet harmony combin'd,
With unaffected grace are so display'd—
The statesman casts not o'er the friend a shade:
Hence is the Muse ambitious of thy name,
T' inspire—to grace—to dignify her theme.

Two miles from *Hounslow*, tow'rds the west is plac'd,
With all the beauties of retirement grac'd,
A grand and rural seat in *Berkeley* fam'd,
Gay *Crantford's* Castle by the Muses nam'd :
Where Health's preserved in unpolluted air ;
Where smiling Peace extirpates ev'ry care ;
Where *Amalthea* holds her golden horn,
And brisk diversions 'wake with ev'ry morn.

From naval toils the hero here retir'd, (*c*)
Smil'd on the glories Victory had acquir'd,
From many tempests—many fights sustain'd,
With dignity enjoy'd what valour gain'd.
Fix'd in the records of undying Fame,
To latest ages lives great *Berkeley's* name.

From him, my lord, such honours you derive,
As a true son of glory still survive ;
Heir of his titles, fortune, every grace,
Requir'd to fill the worthy patriot's place;
As *Aristides* just, with sense refin'd,
Sincere, plain-hearted, and secure of mind;
With Wit well guarded, with Politeness grac'd,
To give society its highest taste.

Here golden Plenty blooms—here sacred Peace
Is always favour'd with a rich increase.
Here all serene, in sweet retirement plac'd,
Life incorrupt, and joys unmix'd you taste.
Thus blest with smiling Heaven's indulgent store,
'Twould scarce be just to ask—to wish for more :
Yet more the Deity propitious gives,
To bless the mansion, where your consort lives ;
Richly improv'd, where native goodness reigns,
And every female grace adorns the scenes.
Smooth as the gentle stream her passions flow ;
Her words the language of her bosom show.

Behold two infant sons of chaste delight,
In every grace, in every beauty bright :
In them may all those excellencies shine,
That have distinguish'd hitherto your line !

Before the front, a swelling river glides ;
A lofty bridge bends o'er its rising sides.

A winding vale the peaceful flood receives;
And here the stream its glassy bosom heaves.
The broad-spread breams, and red-finned roaches here,
With bright-eyed perch, and spangled trout appear:
Dace, gudgeon, golden carp, and silver eel,
The deep recesses of the flood conceal.
Fixing to bearded hooks the treach'rous baits,
With trembling line the patient angler waits.
The springing fish divide the crystal flood,
And leap at death in greedy gust of food.
Clandestine nets the fleaky jack surround,
Prince of the finny troops, that here abound.
In various distant ponds the scaly prey,
All o'er the heath, within their prisons play;
And many streams in winding channels sweep,
To seek insensibly the swelling deep.

  Hence should I wander o'er the southern plain,
Two lonely miles—t' indulge my pensive vein;
I might regale with true benevolence,
With candour, friendship, and with solid sense.* (d)
Thither some few of genius oft retire,
Or blythe or solemn, as their themes inspire.
There with selected, social, honest friends,
The man of taste an evening often spends.
There unreproving mirth, and wit refin'd,
Call decent laughter forth, with temp'rance join'd.

* S——ll U——ll, Esq.

Mechanic art there forms the nitrous grain,
The dread of treach'rous *France* and boastful *Spain.*

Near to the town, behold a spacious course, (*e*)
The scene of trial for the sportive horse.
With tall, white posts the ample circuit's grac'd,
Of equal size at proper distance plac'd.
The neighing coursers pant in ev'ry vein ;
Champ on the bit, and paw the grassy plain.
Stripp'd of their cloths, in order they advance :
Quick beats the drum,—when ardently they prance.
Away they start and sweep the circly mound,
Scarcely imprint the surface of the ground :
With eager speed as swift they stretch along,
The plain rolls back behind the giddy throng.
Th' expanse receives th' alarms of ev'ry heat ;
And echoing vales promiscuous shouts repeat.

Here soar aloft the sweet ætherial train,
And safely wander through the azure plain.
O'er nature's common, free from ev'ry care,
The tuneful songsters skim the passive air.
'Midst dawning clouds the sky-lark mounting sings,
While the gay squadrons plume their painted wings.
The black-bird, whistling on the thorny bush,
Answers the mellow bull-finch, and the thrush.
Join'd in wild concert, then their warbling throats,
Run o'er a sweet variety of notes :
But over all the kind, contending throng,
The tuneful thrush and wood-lark raise their song.

2—2

When nought but balm is breathing thro' the woods,
In evenings mild—when zephyrs curl the floods ;
The nightingale repeats her plaintive song,
In list'ning fancy's ear resounding long.
With soft, mellifluous, melancholy strains,
The sweetly tortur'd heart she entertains.
With sympathetic grief the feather'd throng,
In silence wrapt, admire th' enchanting song,
Sad sitting on some solitary tree,
The wood-dove murmurs out her partner's elegy.

The gaudy-wing'd musicians charm the woods,
While larger wild-fowl sport about the floods.
In safe retreat they on the surface play,
Till from the fowler's view they wing their way.
The wild-ducks, pendant o'er the dimpling stream,
Their mossy domes in artful manner frame.
With scarlet eyes the pheasant often strays,
And whirs across the russet lonely maze.
Long-beak'd Curlieus, and easterlings are seen,
And winding snipes, to flutter o'er the green.
Should some rude foot their heathy haunts molest,
Alarm'd, the mother soon forsakes her nest.
The white wing'd plover wheels her sounding flight ;
Yet keeps her helpless family in sight.

In full career the setter beats the field,
Where circling covies, lurking, lie conceal'd.
In the rough stubbles,—by the tainted gale,
That meets his scent along the ridgy vale.

Alarm'd, with caution struck, out-stretch'd he lies,
With lift-up nose he points the latent prize ;
Until the plumy group entangled beat
With useless, languid wings, the meshy net.
The thund'ring sport of guns are heard around
The dogs, impatient, at the firing bound :
Th' alluring gins, and treach'rous nets no less,
The footed and the feather'd game distress.

Here clam'rous troops of teal and wigeon rise ;
And cackling flocks, like clouds, obscure the skies.
While some, in airy legions, take their flight,
Others, not able to o'ercome the fright,
Leave not their tender and unfeather'd care,
But, flutt'ring round them, hover in the air,
In long excursion, then they wing their way,
To lead the poacher and his dog astray.

When the sky reddens with departing light,
And pearly dews proclaim th' approach of night ;
The clouds with golden edges float along,
And safe retreats conceal the plumy throng.

Here from the heath the black-tail'd moorcock (*f*)
        springs,
And slowly moves his wet incumber'd wings ;
Till from some hostile tube a shower of lead,
Breaks forth in fire and smoke, and strikes him dead.
The shudd'ring pout with wings expanded lies ;
Draws to his breast his feet, and springing dies.

When in the blush of morn fresh breathing gales,
In wanton whispers skim along the vales;
Rous'd by the cock, the soon-drest shepherd (g) leaves
His peaceful cottage—and to pasture drives
His folds, to taste the verdure of the morn;
And farmers rise to guard their ripening corn.

The studious mind starts from the bed of sloth,
T' enjoy the cool and silent hour,—still loth
To lose the time to meditation due,
When ev'ry friendly muse invites him too.
Then his soft lyre the god of seasons sings,
And ev'ry change a change of rapture brings.

Mary,* well harden'd to the morning air,
Now with delight surveys her feather'd care.
With early thrift she tends her home-bred flock
Of cackling pullets round the crested cock;
Where all are pleas'd, and pecking by his side,
And each desirous to become his bride.
If with his happy claws he springs a grain,
He to his fav'rite hen presents the gain;
Yet all with gallant freedom——debonair,
With equal ease, his equal favours share;
And ev'ry morn their grateful tribute pay,
To her that duly feeds them ev'ry day.

The ducks and geese upon the liquid plain,
Move slow before their downy, chirping train,

* Any farmer's wife.

Protective of their new-hatch'd tender young,
With watchful eye, superb they sail along :
With equal care, the hardy turkeys hatch ;
With equal pains their puny brood they watch.
The redd'ning cock, with strides and threatenings loud,
Chudders defiance,—looks as *Cæsar* proud,
The gaudy peacock spreads his various tail,
And seems in awful majesty to sail.

When night's involving shade bids *Hodge** repair
Homeward, from penning up his fleecy care ;
Or from the labours of the wounded field,
(Where nature's genial bounty lies conceal'd)
Or when to fodder, from the naked plain,
He whistling drives his dumb, discerning train ;
After a plain refreshment he revives,
And to divert his tender offspring strives,
He drinks his pot of home-brew'd ale, and smokes ⎫
A cheerful pipe,—tells twenty merry jokes ; ⎬
And lives as pleasantly as richer folks. ⎭
His little children climb, in sweet amaze,
About his neck ; and, while they fondly gaze,
With innocent delight his stories hear,
And quite impatient of th' event appear.
To please him is the good wife's chief employ ;
Her early comfort, and her evening joy.
With faithful love, and innocent delight,
The day's fatigue is recompens'd at night.

* Any farmer or shepherd.

Thus chequer'd is their life—they daily share,
True pleasure mingled with a frugal care.

When reeds scarce rustle with the balmy breeze,
Soft as the humming sounds of distant bees ;
When of the sun a long extended blaze,
Upon the water's quiv'ring surface plays ;
And, when beyond the golden verge of day,
Mild evenings their soft, dusky wings display ;
Sometimes the flagelet, or violin's strains,
Invite the nymphs to dance upon the plains ;
Who graceful on the level verdure move
In varied measures—innocence and love
Dilate their spirits ; while the cooling breeze,
That gently whispers through th' embow'ring trees,
Their flowing garments swell—fans ev'ry breast,
And wanton sighs on ev'ry rising chest.
Exulting joy, with love, in soft disguise,
Distends their hearts, and flashes in their eyes.
Promiscuous cheerfulness they all display,
And quite forget the labours of the day.

In higher life, the evenings often pass,
With a gay pipe and recreating glass ;
In sober mirth, improving, blythe and gay,
The happy minutes sweetly glide away.
From hospitality new ardours rise,
And sparkling wine the distant sun supplies.
A train of brisk diversions crown the day,
And cheerful nights in pleasure steal away.

Each hand's employ'd, while thus an hour we pass;
While one supports the pipe, one fills the glass.
A copious bowl the shaggy leaf contains;
A pendant* globe the oily moisture drains:
A suction bland the glowing weed obeys,
And through a spiral tube the blast conveys.
Th' expanding vapour spreads o'er all the room,
And warms its bosom with a rich perfume.

   Hail useful weed! a treasure not the least,
To thought most friendly—grateful to the taste!
Besides thy healing influence and use,
Thou add'st a flavour to the purple juice.

   When *Boreas* spreads with sleet the stiff'ning plains,
And seizes nature in its icy chains;
The sprightly youth their sportive task renew
Th' enliv'ning, though laborious, course pursue;
And track the footsteps of the circling hare,
Nipp'd with the keenness of the freezing air.
Yet exercise gives—colour to the skin,
Warmth to the vital streams that flow within;
Strength to the sinews, vigour to the nerves,
And all the system properly preserves.

   With poles equipp'd, the nimble lads convene,
And in light habits all approach the scene.
A sense of joy their speaking eyes proclaim,
And all impatient seem to start the game.

   * This description is designed for a glass pipe.

O'er hills and vales, and through th' awaken'd woods,
O'er dreary wilds, and through meandering floods,
With every nerve the hardy swain pursues,
And eagerness of toil his strength renews.
Many a shift poor puss is forc'd to make,
Yet few the circles she's allow'd to take.
Adhesive to the track, the grey-hounds bend,
And to her heels their lengthen'd snouts extend;
While she, uncertain whether caught or no,
Springs from the gripe, and cheats the treach'rous foe.
So close they bear upon the flying prey,
With fear—with force o'ercome, she dies away.
Unfairly press'd, the sharp-nos'd murd'rers seize
Th' unequal match'd—the meanly destin'd prize.

When early twilight temperate is found,
And neither frost nor floods oppress the ground;
Hunting, the first of rural brisk delights,
To manly toils the youthful breast invites.

Proceed, my muse, the generous task pursue,
From *Crantford-Field* take thy unbounded view;
In graphic lays declare what pleasures reign,
And what diversions crowd the lively scene!

Here, when the rosy dawn brings on the day,
And blended sweets appear in foliage gay,
(Ere *Sol* or *Myra* leave their balmy bed,
While pleasing dreams amuse each female's head;
While o'er their pillows soft chimeras creep,
And make them smile at conquests in their sleep).

In search of game here lively sportsmen meet,
And every bush, and every furrow beat ;
Explore the latent tracts of every field,
Try what the lawns and what the coverts yield.

    When the skill'd huntsman, after a survey,
Of each *purlieu*, has singled out his prey ;
Soon as the rustling of the shrubs she hears,
And quick advancing steps, puss pricks her ears,
Hark, hark to Tunewell, hark !　Away she goes,
And makes a scoff of her insulting foes.
When sweet-tongued *Ruler* leads the crying crew,
How fleet and close do all the rest pursue !
    Hot-steaming *Driver, Silver, Darling, Tatler,*
Vocif'rate *Fowler, Fav'rite, Coral, Rattler ;*
Fortune and *Violet, Toss-pot, Fumy, Tipler,*
Careless and *Blossom, Merry-lass* and *Fiddler ;*
Tulip and *Wanton, Damsel, Juno, Bowman,*
Cupid and *Dido, Tanner, Lady, Rowman ;*
Quick-scented *Flora, Comely, Light-foot, Nancy ;*
Phœnix and *Seamstress, Ruby, Tulip, Dancy ;*
Whipster and *Cloudy ;* and, to crown the scene,
Let us bring *Doxy,* and old *Piper* in.
The tawny group is too prolix for rhyme,
And too encroaching on my reader's time.

    The frighten'd wand'rer often shifts her rounds,
To shun the malice of the greedy hounds ;
Who now in vain their rage and speed renew,
In vain the distant, *doubling* hare pursue.

The magic horn calls in the long-ear'd pack,
Unrav'ling by degrees her faithless track.
To fenny marshes then their course they bend,
And o'er the vast expanse their voice extend,
When *puss* the *harriers* hard behind her spies,
Couched on the sod, in doubt she closely lies ;
And, as they, *tufting,** sweep along the field,
She *squatting,* lies beneath the fern conceal'd :
Then straight makes off to some adjacent moss,
The dogs o'ershoot their game and come t'a loss.
As they're call'd back, the busy huntsman lights,
To *prick* the *puss,* and *put his dogs to rights ;*
First *draws his hounds a compass round about,*
Then strictly *beats the ground, to tread her out.*

Forbear, my muse, to tell the sportsman's fears,
Or what dejection in his looks appears ;
What great impatience labours in his breast ;
What peevish doubts his longing heart molest :
But gently condescend to hide his grief,
And soothe his mind with unforeseen relief.

Now, while the dogs are thus upon the scent,
They all disperse, to try the way she went.
The snarling pack, being *cast* to search about,
Staunch *Rockwood hunts the ground,* and finds her out.
Some happy eye takes up the distant game,
With loud *holloos* from every voice proclaim.

* When an hound, holding up his nose, takes the scent of corn, fern, rushes, or heath.

When thus we have the dear *recovery made*,
In ev'ry face a cheerful air's display'd,
Hoaks, hark to music—ev'ry vale rebounds,
And *to the finders throw off all the hounds*.
The distant rocks obey the jovial cries,
'Midst thickets, which in gay confusion rise.
The steady dogs are *branching** all around ;
Reverberating hills the shouts rebound.
The valleys speak with voices not their own ;
And echo answers in a fainter tone.
In vain to climb the rugged heights she tries,
In vain to covert from the dogs she flies ;
While in full cry they all increase her dread,
And hard behind the foaming horses tread.
Tracer for scent, and *Spie* renown'd for speed,
Black-foot and *Climb-cliff*, all of *Wiltshire* breed,
With eager haste pursue the tim'rous prey ;
And, sweeping on, or find or make a way :
Until with stiff'ning limbs the fainting hare,
Run fairly down, in death dissolves her fear.
The foremost rider triumphs in the prize,
And strikes with joyful shouts the vaulted skies.
From ev'ry wound springs forth a purple flood,
Spouts in his face, and stains his hands with blood.
Then the tir'd *hunters* all abate their speed ;
And by the *vocal tube* her death's decreed.

* When an hound, holding up his nose, takes the scent of a
tree or shrub.

The jolly huntsman, loaded with the slain,
Returns in triumph from the echoing plain.

How far superior are the rural sports,
To ease inglorious, or the toil of courts!
From these proceeds an indolence supine,
From those arises all that's masculine.
When verdant glades afford a lively hue,
And the gay lawns are spangled o'er with dew;
Soon as the glance from mild *Aurora's* eyes,
With crimson smiles adorns the streaky skies:
Fresh, hearty sportsmen, oft surround the wood,
With tuneful horn, with hounds and hunters good;
Here *storm the thicket* and the craggy rocks,
And soon unkennel here the wily fox.*
The prowling cub starts furious from his den,
And scorns the cries of dogs and shouts of men.
The op'ning hounds are fir'd—they snuff and vent,
And trace his footsteps, eager of the scent.
With what prelusive joy they hail the morn,
And with what harmony obey the horn.
Thus rous'd, away the wakeful savage bounds,
Until his ears have lost the wounding sounds.
Exulting then he takes the distant moor,
And in his cunning thinks himself secure.

* *N.B.* The Chace, a Poem subjoined to an Essay intituled,
The Pleasures and Advantages of Female Literatures, (printed
in *London*, 1741, and to be sold by Messrs. *Manby* and *Cox* on
Ludgate Hill) was written by the same author.

A froth besmears his grinning chops around,
And, as he runs along, befoams the ground.
Each hungry dog the length'ning chace pursues,
And snuffs the vapour from the tainted dews ;
Till, in united cry, they shoot away,
And in full stretch bear on the bounding prey.
Crowner and *Rebel*, *Kilbuck*, *Drunkard*, *Stroler*,
Topper and *Ringwood*, *Plowman*, *Bouncer*, *Joler;*
Vulcan and *Thumper*, *Snowball*, *Ranter*, *Gipsy*,
Farmer and *Steamer*, *Trueman*, *Jilter*, *Tipsy;*
Fine-spotted *Dainty*, *Fill-pot*, *Jewel*, *Rover*,
With long-breath'd *Ranger*, *Dancer*, *Beauty*, *Clover*,
And many others (all I cannot name),
Still follow, with unequal pace, the game.
With prick'd up ears, the hunters then renew,
Instinctive courage, and the chace pursue.
Their turgid nerves they swell, they snort and blow,
And whitening foam upon the verdure throw.
The woods, the valleys, and the concave sky,
Both earth and air are fill'd with harmony.
When once poor *Reynard* sees himself inclos'd,
By horses, men, and hostile dogs oppos'd ;
When thus he finds his dangers all renew'd,
By all forsaken, and by foes pursu'd.
Strait to the stream (when neither speed nor force,
Nor all his craft avail) he bends his course.
Even there the dogs pursue him through the flood,
And nought will quench their thirst but *Reynard's*
    blood ;

" *Who, like a felon, conscious of his guilt,*
" *Is forc'd to bleed, where he much blood hath spilt.*"
The deep-tun'd horn his sentence then declares,
And *Reynard* to resist no longer dares.
Indignant, with disdainful grin, he dies,
And malice flashes from his fiery eyes.

The ROYAL SISTERS (*h*) visit oft these plains,
And condescend to grace the sportive scenes.
Soon as the mounting lark awakes the dawn,
And sweetly warbles o'er the silver'd lawn;
Convening sportsmen with the cheerful horn,
Alarm their dogs, and hail the rosy morn.
The stag, *from cover broke*, begins to view
The threat'ning dangers, that his fears renew;
Still half amaz'd looks round, yet held by fear,
Can scarce believe his enemies so near.
He calls his strength and vigour to his aid;
But yet his fears more powerfully persuade.
Being thus betray'd, the dire alarm he takes,
And his unfaithful keeper straight forsakes.
Enrag'd away he bounds, or rather flies,
A while pursu'd but by the hunter's eyes.
All view the game with envy from afar,
Eager to follow in the *sylvan* war.
Melodious op'nings charm the sportsmen's ears,
Sweeter than all the music of the spheres.
Royal AMELIA (*i*)—goddess of the plain,
Begin the chace, and crown the joyous scene!

When to the field this graceful princess leads
A youthful train of honourable maids ;
And troops of lovely dames are seen to ride,
In form and shape majestic by her side ;
AMELIA —— princess of that lovely train,
From all the rest must adoration gain ;
Such graces through her whole demeanour shine,
In beauty—majesty—and air divine.

The stag (*k*) thus singled from the butting throng,
With all his strength united, sweeps along.
Resolv'd the paths of danger now to tread,
At his scorn'd *shelter* shakes his beamy head ;
Which, like a tree with leafless branches drest,
Bespeaks the boldness rising in his breast :
But soon—too soon his wav'ring spirits droop,
And he to coward fear resigns all hope.
He starts—consults his feet—and, gazing round,
He turns his dappled face to every sound.
The gath'ring noise invades his wakeful ears ;
The shouts of men, with dogs, increase his fears.
Against the breeze he darts, or seems to fly ;
But still pursu'd by the malicious cry,
Bursts through the thickets—glances through the
        woods,
And plunges deep into the widest floods.
Deafen'd and stunn'd with the promiscuous noise,
The kennel's concert all his peace annoys ;

3

Till he at length to rudest shades repairs,
To seek for safety, and to soothe his cares.
Now, though the greedy dogs him overtake,
" *Yet save his life for fair* AMELIA'S *sake.*"
In this retirement let him live conceal'd,
Until his strength—until his fears be heal'd :
Leave him among his savage slaves to rove,
While all the herd obedient to him move ;
" There let him think again on empire and on love."

When the diversions of the field are o'er,
And exercise fatigues than pleases more ;
Convey me, goddess, to the western end
Of *Hounslow Town*—to see a worthy friend.
There all excesses are alike disdain'd ;
With ease polite, there all are entertain'd.
With calm delight, and pity hence we view,
The gloomy cares that busy men pursue ;
Where each by diff'rent ways attempts to gain,
Uncertain happiness with certain pain :
Whilst we, serene, th' exalted raptures know,
Which from content, and sweet retirement flow.
Here female management its worth displays ;
Here just economy demands our praise.

Clara! propitious to my pleasing toil,
Let me your gentle ear engage a while ;
Let me with truth—with decent pride extol,
What even envy dares not flatt'ry call !

In soft assemblage join'd, your virtues shine ;
They grace my song—inspirit every line.
With fame unblemish'd ; with the tend'rest breast,
Studious to heal the cares of the distrest ;
With cheerful ease you ev'ry sorrow calm,
And to their well search'd wounds apply the balm ;
On true beneficence your thoughts employ,
To make the hopeless heart exult for joy.
In you the human graces all unite——
All in your conduct glow with beauteous light.
If candour, and sincerity of mind,
With ease polite—with piety refin'd,
With friendship affable—benevolence,
With wit—with goodness, and with social sense,
With ev'ry excellence approv'd above,
Can claim esteem, and universal love ;
Can crown your sex with honours all mature,
Can present peace and future bliss secure ;
Just is your challenge to fair virtue's fame,
And to eternal joys as just your claim.

The twisted horn, with bold enlivening strains,
Here wakes the echoes from the distant plains
The voice, spinnet, bass, violin, and flute,
In tones concordant one another suit.
Each busy hand, their sev'ral parts assign'd,
Fill up the choir, in harmony combin'd.
The pliant quills, and bright metallic strings,
Obey the gentle touch while *Celia* sings ;

And, while her flying fingers touch the lyre,
The mellow notes seraphic joys inspire.
Fix'd in each breast the flowing concord dwells,
And ev'ry faculty with rapture swells.
United breathes such soul-dissolving airs,
That ev'ry list'ning heart forgets all cares.
Her warbling voice deceives the feasted ear,
We think her singing still, and listen still to hear.

Meanwhile the *sire* his well-tun'd fiddle tries,
Commands the changing notes to fall and rise :
The trembling chords transportingly obey,
And charm the ears with each melodious lay :
The thrilling, sprightly sounds, that some create,
Others more hoarse responsively repeat.
The soft, the shrill, the deep, the slow,
In sweet variety of numbers flow.
Each swelling tone inflicts a pleasing wound,
And ev'ry fair drinks in th' inspiring sound.
The nice compulsion all disarm'd obey,
And drive our cares in pure delight away,
All by confed'rate symphonies impart,
Such modulated airs, to warm the heart,
As shake the passions, from the various string,
And joy extatic to each organ bring.
Sweetly confus'd, our friendly transports rise,
Start from their tongue and kindle in our eyes.
Our spirits, through the new-strung nerves refine,
And dart ideas to the soul—divine.

Celestial raptures harmony reveals—
Enchanting music's force all nature feels.
Each thrilling grace attracts our ravish'd ears,
And by degrees alleviates all our cares :
The num'rous strains so sweetly pleasing flow,
In all our minds there's not a place for woe.
Music, delightful, glides into the soul,
Elates the spirits—ravishes the whole :
Refines the passions, and extends the heart,
Awak'ning ev'ry nerve with strokes of art.
O'er all the scene joy spreads her golden wings,
And ev'ry *overture* new rapture brings.

At length a jocund bottle crowns the day,
To keep our spirits debonair and gay.
Again we traverse o'er the *sylvan* scene,
The game revive and kill it o'er again.
With sprightly glee promiscuously relate,
How clean our hunters leap'd o'er such a gate ;
How hard they drove—how light they trod the moor,
How bold we rid, and in our course how sure ;
Soon as uncoupled, how they spread abroad,
To try his scent each dog a diff'rent road ;
When *puss* first left her *seat*,* what shifts she made,
How long she *dodg'd*, how with the hounds she play'd.
How oft she squatted, and what means she found,
To bring her back to her accustom'd ground ;

* The place where a hare sits in the day-time, is called her
seat or form.

How close sometimes the *doubling* jade did lie,
Until the dewlap'd dogs had pass'd her by ;
How she to her *relief* (*a*) skulk'd to her *form,*
How *Sporter thrust her up* from 'midst the corn ;
How such *an harle* (*b*) of *hounds* a *vaunt-lay* (*c*) made,
O'er the *crotills* (*d*) how other *bablers* (*e*) play'd ;
How oft the dogs were forc'd to *hunt the foil* (*f*).
How oft puss *vaulted,* (*g*) and how oft *took soil ;* (*h*)
How *Blueman* (*i*) *ran the heel,* (*k*) how *Piper bawl'd,*
How *Rival flourish'd* (*l*) when the *scent was cold ;*
How *Captain cried the game* (*m*), how *Whipster* led,
Maugre the heavy *trash* (*n*) so near his head.

(*a*) The place where a hare keeps all night is called her relief.

(*b*) A couple and a half, or a pair of couples ; two of them buckled together is an harle of hounds.

(*c*) When hounds are thrown off at game, before other hounds that are hunting the same game come up, it is called a vaunt-lay.

(*d*) The ordure or dung of an hare.

(*e*) Hounds that give their mouths too busily, and not upon the scent.

(*f*) When hounds hunt where they have run before.

(*g*) Going to earth in a rock or hole.

(*h*) When a hare goes into the water.

(*i*) When a hound runs the scent backward, meaning the contrary way, he runs the heel or runs counter.

(*k*) When a hound gives his mouth, going to the field or in the field, before he has found the scent, he bawls.

(*l*) When a hound feels a cold scent, and does not cry it, he flourishes.

(*m*) When a hound first finds the scent and opens, he cries it, or challenges it.

(*n*) Any thing fastened to the neck of a fleet hound in the

This gives a relish to th' impurpled juice,
That gently flows through ev'ry vital sluice.
With correspondent fires our bosoms move :
We end the night as we began, in love.
Thus free from strife, corroding care, and noise,
Retirement feasts us with untainted joys.

---

time of his hunting, to abate his speed, and make him keep
company with slower hounds. A piece of stiff leather, tied to a
coller, makes a good trash.

BOOKS printed for the AUTHOR.

1. AN Essay on the Existence of a God, published, price 1s. 6d. all sold.

2. An History of the State of Man, with regard to Religion and Morals; from the beginning of the World to the Reformation: sold by Messrs. *Manby* and *Cox* on *Ludgate Hill,* and *T. Gardner* at *Cowley's* Head in the *Strand*, Price 4s. unbound.

3. A Letter of genteel and moral Advice, to a young Lady, &c., the 5th Edition, price 1s. 6d. unbound; sold by *Charles Hitch*, in *Paternoster Row*.

4. An Essay on the Pleasures and Advantages of Female Literature. Price 1s. sold by Messrs. *Manby* and *Cox* on *Ludgate Hill*.

5. The Humours of the *Black Dog,* approved by the late eminent DEAN SWIFT, the 10th edition, after seventeen thousand being sold, price 6d., ready for the press.

6. Rural Felicity compared with Public Life; a *Doric* poem, ready for the press, price 1s.

All these books are sold by the AUTHOR.

NOTES.

NOTE (a) p. 9.

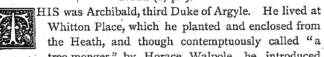

THIS was Archibald, third Duke of Argyle. He lived at Whitton Place, which he planted and enclosed from the Heath, and though contemptuously called "a tree-monger" by Horace Walpole, he introduced many foreign trees and shrubs into this country, which by the beauty of their forms and colours have greatly contributed to the pleasing effect of the English landscape. From an old engraved plan of Whitton, in my possession, it was surrounded on all sides by the Heath, but the east, where the Duke had his nursery. Almost every tree at Whitton was raised from seed, planted by the Duke in 1724. And we can have, from that circumstance, a very good idea of the growth of trees according to their age. The girths of the two largest cedars at Mr. Gostling's in 1810, at three feet from the ground, were exactly eleven feet four inches. In the part then rented by Mr. Hobhouse, one cedar measured twelve feet one inch and a half, another eleven feet eleven inches. On the plan is the horizontal wind-engine for raising the water which then surrounded the grounds. The Gothic tower, erected by the Duke, the fish ponds, bowling green, orange walk, aviary, &c., are all laid down with careful precision. The circular spot planted with trees in the old nursery, on the right hand side of the road leading to Hounslow from Whitton, is called the Rabbit Warren, and in its centre was a Chinese summer-house. After the Duke's death, the estate was purchased by George Gostling, Esq., a Proctor of Doctors Commons, who divided the pleasure grounds, and sold the part containing the late Duke's house, to Sir William Chambers, the well known architect of Somerset House. The noble conservatory built by the Duke was then converted into the elegant villa now known as Whitton House, upon the pediment of which is a bas relief after the antique, representing the destruction of the Titans by Jupiter. It was executed by Dere, an artist of great promise, who, alas! died too young to take his place in the annals of fame. After the decease of Sir William Chambers, Whitton Place was inhabited for a time by Sir B. Hobhouse, M.P. At last Mr. Gostling re-purchased the part of the estate formerly sold by him, pulled down Whitton Place, reserving Whitton House as his residence.

Before the Duke attained to his highest title, he was known as the Marquis of Islay, and the following epigram upon him, on cutting a vista at Whitton, was written by Horace Walpole :—

" Old Islay to show his fine delicate taste
    In improving his gardens purloined from the waste,
    Bade his gardener one day to open his views,
    By cutting a couple of grand avenues.
    No particular prospect his lordship intended,
    But left it to chance how his walks should be ended.
    With transport and joy he beheld his first view end
    In a favourite prospect—a church that was ruined.
    But alas! what a sight did the next cut exhibit—
    At the end of the walk hung a rogue on a gibbet.
    He beheld it and wept, for it caused him to muse on
    Full many a Campbell that died with his shoes on.
    All amazed and aghast at the ominous scene,
    He ordered it quick to be closed up again
    With a clump of Scotch firs, that served for a screen."

In early life Sir William Chambers made a voyage to China, and he was ever after impressed with the beauties of the Chinese style of gardening. With these views he built the Pagoda in Kew Gardens, and wrote a *Dissertation on Oriental Gardening*. This was enough for the wits of the day, and there immediately afterwards appeared, *An Heroic Epistle to Sir William Chambers, Knight, Comptroller General of His Majesty's Works, and Author of a late Dissertation on Oriental Gardening, enriched with explanatory Notes, chiefly extracted from that elaborate Performance*. This, we know now, was written by Mason, and in it we find the following lines :—

> " Now to our lawns of dalliance and delight,
> Join we the groves of horror and affright ;
> This to achieve, no foreign aids we try,
> Thy gibbets, Bagshot, shall our wants supply ;
> Hounslow, whose heath sublimer terror fills,
> Shall with her gibbets lend her powder mills."

The explanatory note extracted from Sir William Chambers's *Dissertation*, and applied to these lines is —

"Their scenes of terror are composed of gloomy woods, &c., gibbets, crosses, wheels, and the whole apparatus of torture are seen from the roads. Here, too, they conceal in cavities, on the summits of the highest mountains, founderies, lime-kilns, and glass works, which send forth large volumes of flame, and continued columns of thick smoke, that give to these mountains the appearance of volcanoes." To this the satirist adds —" Now, to produce both these effects, viz., the appearance of volcanoes and earthquakes, we have here substituted the occasional explosion of a powder mill, which (if there be not too much simplicity in the contrivance) it is apprehended will at once answer all the purposes of lime-kilns and electrical machines, and imitate thunder and the explosions of cannon into the bargain."

We learn from Brewer's *Middlesex* that one powder mill at

Hounslow was thrice blown up, killing fourteen people, in the year 1796. And it is with grief, we are compelled to say, that the Hounslow Powder Mills still maintain their unenviable notoriety for frequent and fatal explosions.

We see from Rocque's Map of Middlesex, published in 1754, shortly after this poem was written, that the gibbets stood on the point of land formed by the junction of the Bath and Staines roads. Wilkes, however, had too much taste to introduce into his poem such disagreeable subjects as gibbets. In the first volume of the *Asylum for Fugitive Pieces*, published in 1785, there is the following :—

FAMILIAR VERSES ADDRESSED TO TWO YOUNG GENTLEMEN
AT THE HOUNSLOW ACADEMY.

" Take notice, roguelings, I prohibit,
   Your walking underneath yon gibbet ;
   Have you not heard, my little ones,
   Of *Raw Head and Bloody Bones ?*
   How do you know but that there fellow,
   May step down quick, and you up swallow ?" ·

The Academy at Hounslow was held in Albemarle House, where the boys always had the *humanising* spectacle of the gibbet before their eyes. There is an engraving extant of it, a copy of which is in the British-Museum. It is dated in 1804, when all England was in arms to resist the threatened invasion of Buonaparte, and represents a spacious play-ground at the back of the house, with all the boys exercising as volunteers.

Though Hounslow Heath was a noted place for highwaymen, many persons were brought there and gibbeted, whose crimes and punishments had taken place at far distant places. Thus, one Theodore Gardelle, a native of Geneva, and an artist, who committed a horrible murder on his landlady, a Mrs. King in Leicester Square, and attempted to dispose of the body under revolting circumstances, was hanged in the Haymarket, close to Panton Street, and his body was taken down on the same day, the 4th of April, 1761, and hung in chains on Hounslow Heath.

The gibbets were at last removed on account of the passage of the royal family this way to Windsor. We cannot tell the exact date, but it was previous to 1809, when Hughson's *Circuit of London* was published.

NOTE (*b*), p. 15.

I have often fondly thought that the two old elms, still standing opposite the Bell public-house, were the remnants of those trees. But Wilkes expressly states that they were " behind the town ," and according to Rocque's Map of 1754, they were about thirty yards down the Bell Lane on the way to Whitton.

NOTE (*c*), p. 16.

James Earl of Berkeley, Vice Admiral of Great Britain.

NOTE (*d*), p. 18.

This was Samuel Underhill, whose death is recorded in the *London Magazine*, as occurring on the 18th September, 1762. The " nitrous grain " was then, as it still is, a dread nearer home than to " treacherous France," or " boastful Spain." A cutting of an old newspaper, in my possession, of the 29th of December, 1758, relates that about twelve o'clock at night, a store of gunpowder at the mills belonging to Samuel Underhill, Esq., took fire. The quantity of powder then drying was great, consisting of seventeen hundredweight, and the explosion was extremely violent and alarming, insomuch that Mr. Underhill's dwelling-house was considerably damaged, though at near three hundred yards distance from the works.

NOTE (*e*), p. 19.

The site of the race-course is clearly laid down on Rocque's map of Middlesex. It was on the left of the Staines road, a short distance from the Bell public-house. Many notices of the races at Hounslow are found in the newspapers of the last century, as the following, from the *Evening Post* of July 20, 1734:—

" On Thursday last, seven horses started at the races on Hounslow Heath, viz., Mr. Clarke's mare *Fair Rosamond*, Mr. Riley's horse *White Stockings*, Mr. How's horse *Stradler*, Mr. Clavering's horse *Harmless*, Mr. Pathson's mare *Milkmaid*, Mr. Major's horse *Squirrel*, and Mr. Selby's mare *Molly Mogg*, for the Give and Take Purse, which was won by Mr. Riley's *White Stockings*. They ran three heats ; Mr. Riley's horse won the first and last heats, and Mr. Clarke's *Fair Rosamond* got the second heat, and broke her leg running the last heat. Mr. Pathson's grey mare *Milkmaid*, and Mr. Major's black horse *Squirrel*, were distanced the first heat."

On July 23rd, 1734, in the same paper we may read that :—

" On Friday at the races on Hounslow Heath, five horses started for the Purse of £20, viz., Mr. Smith's chesnut mare *Favourite*, Mr. Newman's bay horse *Dimple*, Mr. Lawrence's bay mare *Penelope*, Sir Rowland Symond's black horse *Jubilee Dick*, and the Lord Anne Hamilton's mare, who was entered at the post, and won the plate."

Lord Anne Hamilton was a curious instance of a feminine name being attached to a man ; he was christened after Queen Anne.

" On Saturday, at the said races, five horses started for the Hunter's £20 Purse, viz., Mr. Hammond's chesnut horse *Foreigner*, Mr. Proctor's grey horse *Careless Tom*, Mr. Colvin's bay gelding *Splint*, Mr. Upson's sorrel gelding *Fox Hunter*, and Mr. Newman's bay mare *Silver Hair*, which was won with great ease by Mr. Colvin's bay gelding."

NOTE (*f*), p. 21.

The moorcock (*Tetrao tetrix*) is not now, nor has it been for many years, a native of the Heath. Though there may be found

a few specimens of the bird on the Surrey Hills, their nearest
habitat is Hampshire.

NOTE (*g*), p. 22.

Wilkes has here taken the whole idea from Thomson, and ex-
pressed it in almost the very same words as the poet of the
Seasons, who says :—

> " Rous'd by the cock, the soon-clad shepherd leaves,
> His mossy cottage, where with Peace he dwells ;
> And from the crowded fold, in order, drives
> His flock, to taste the verdure of the morn."

Thomson was then alive at Richmond, or had just died.

NOTE (*h*), p. 32.

The Princess Amelia and Caroline, daughters of George the
Second. In 1733, they brought the well of Islington Spa, then
called New Tunbridge Wells, into fashion, from their going
thither to drink the waters. In the *Humours of New Tunbridge
Wells*, the poet asks in astonishment what has brought such
great company there :—

> " Whence comes it that the shining great,
> To titles born and awful state,
>   Thus condescend, thus check their will ;
> And scud away to Tunbridge Wells,
> To mix with vulgar beaux and belles ?
> Ye sages your famed glasses raise,
> Survey this meteor's dazzling blaze,
>   And say portends it good or ill "

In a short poem, called *Modern Diversions*, published in the
Universal Magazine, 1753, there is the following verse :—

> " To operas, assemblies,
> Or to a masquerade,
> New Tunbridge, or to Kendal House,
> And this shall be the trade.

We'll sally out to breakfast,
And hear the fiddlers play ;
And there we'll revel, feast, and dance,
And make a merry day.
 For a roving we will go, will go, will go,
  For a roving we will go."

In the *Daily Advertiser* of April 4, 1750, we find the following notice of Kendal House :—

" For certain, Kendal House, Isleworth, near Brentford, Middlesex, eight miles from London, will open for breakfasting on Monday, the 16th inst. The long room for dancing is upwards of sixty feet long, and wide in proportion ; all the other rooms are elegantly fitted up. The orchestra on the water is allowed by all that have seen it, to be in the genteelest taste, being built an octagon, in the Corinthian order, above fifty feet diameter, having an upper and a lower gallery, where gentlemen and ladies may divert themselves with fishing, the canal being well stocked with tench, carp, and all sorts of fish, in great plenty ; near which are two wildernesses, with delightful rural walks ; and through the garden runs a rapid river, shaded with a pleasant grove of trees, with various walks so designed by nature, that in the hottest days of summer you are secured from the heat of the sun. This small but just account of the place falls greatly short of its real beauties. Great care will be taken to keep out all disorderly people. There is a man-cook, and a good larder ; all things as cheap or cheaper than at any place of the kind. Public breakfasts are held on Wednesdays and Fridays."

There is a *Perspective View of Kendall House, near Isleworth,* drawn by Chatelain in 1756, in the British Museum. It represents, most probably, one of these grand public breakfast days. A large orchestra, filled with musicians, is discoursing sweet music, while a number of ladies and gentlemen, the former dressed in hoops and sacs, are walking about ; some amusing themselves with fishing.

The site of Kendal House is well known. It was on the north
side of the road leading from Twickenham to London ; and was
so called from having been the residence of Madame Schulen-
berg, one of the mistresses of George I., who created her
Duchess of Kendal. It was in this house that the " Maypole,"
as this chaste addition to our English aristocracy was irreve-
rently called by the people, fancied that she was visited by the
ghost of the King, in the form of a raven.

There was an earlier house, however, of the same description,
opened at Isleworth. From a cutting of the *General Evening
Post*, May, 1734, in my possession, I extract the following advertisement —

" ISLEWORTH ASSEMBLY.

" Held last year at Dunton House in Isleworth, will begin this
year on Wednesday, the 29th of May, and continue every Wednesday during the season. Subscriptions are taken at Dunton
House.

" N.B.—No persons will be admitted unless introduced by a
subscriber."

The site of Dunton House I have been unable to discover ; it
most probably took its name from a Richard Downton, who,
from a minute of the vestry of Isleworth parish, received with
his wife in 1661, a license to eat flesh in Lent for the " recovery
of their health." And a monument to his second son, also
called Richard Downton, who died in 1711, is on the north wall
of Isleworth Church.

NOTE (*i*), p. 32.

The Princess Amelia, daughter of George II., was born at the
palace of Herenhausen in Hanover, in 1711, and died, the last
survivor of his children, in 1786. She was very fond of hunting,
and all her tastes being decidedly masculine, it is said that she
spent the greater part of the time in her stables. She never
married, but she carried on a strong flirtation with Charles Fitz-
roy, the second Duke of Richmond, and grandson of Charles II.

4

They were in the constant habit of hunting together three days
in the week during the season, and the princess gave great offence
to her mother Queen Caroline, by retiring with the duke on one
occasion from the hunting-field to a house in Windsor Forest,
where they remained long enough to afford ground for scandal.

Later in life she seems to have half unsexed herself by the
masculine tastes that she had imbibed, and the strange attire
which she wore. There is at Hardwicke in Derbyshire, a portrait of her, in a round hat and laced coat, which it is difficult
to believe could have been intended for a woman. Her great
nephew, George the Fourth, when Prince of Wales, used to relate
a rather amusing anecdote at her expense. One cold day, he
said, he was driving with Lord Clermont in the neighbourhood
of Bagshot, when the singular appearance of the Irish Earl, who
was wrapped up in a white great-coat and a kind of flannel hood
over his head, so nearly resembled that of the Princess, that he
was occasionally mistaken for her by the persons who met them
on the road. More than once the princess overheard the following remark :—" What a kind young man the prince must be to
be so attentive to his deaf old aunt !"

For as she increased in years she became exceedingly deaf
and short-sighted, but as Walpole observes, such was the natural
quickness of her perceptions that she seemed to hear and see
better than those whom she conversed with. She never went to
Court after George III. succeeded to the throne, who hated her
with all the energy his weak mind was capable of. Her great
weakness was high play at cards, and she may have exclaimed
with the poet :—

> " At the groom porter's battered bullies play ;
> Some dukes at Mary Bone bowl time away.
> But who the bowl, or rattling dice compares,
> To Basset's heavenly joys, and pleasing cares."

This penchant rendered her especially obnoxious to the mother.

of George III., who used to bitterly complain of her sister-in-law for playing publicly for such high stakes at the rooms at Bath. But Amelia, if she did play cards in a public room, never allowed the slightest encroachment on her dignity, as a great king's daughter. On one occasion, when playing at Bath, a general officer, with presumptive ill-breeding, took a pinch of snuff out of her enormous gold snuff-box, which constantly lay open on the table beside her. The Princess, in a very pointed manner, showed her sense of the liberty thus taken by desiring one of her attendants to throw the box with its contents into the fire.

A contemporary of the Princess, one Mr. Perkins, writing from Bath to Lord Chancellor Hardwick, in 1752, says :—

" Her Royal Highness is very affable and civil ; comes to the room at noon, and sometimes at nights, and plays at cards there, chiefly commerce. She takes all opportunities, when fair, of getting on horseback, and amuses herself almost every day some hours in angling in the river, in a summer-house by the river side in the garden, formerly known by the name of Harrison's Walks, which has two fire-places in it ; and to secure her against cold, puts on a riding-habit and a black velvet postilion's cap tied under her chin."

NOTE (*k*), p. 33.

Hounslow Heath was a favourite hunting ground for the royal family, in George the Second's time, as the following newspaper cuttings in my possession amply testify.

" Yesterday morning their Majesties, the Prince of Wales, the Duke, and eldest Princesses, went to Hounslow Heath, where a stag being turned out at the starting-post, afforded them a pleasant chase for several hours, and taking cross the country towards Hertfordshire, their Majesties followed as far as Harrow-on-the-Hill, and then came back to Kensington, which they did without their attendants, having lost them in the chase. Their Royal Highnesses the Prince, and Duke, pursued the stag, and did not return till late in the afternoon."—*August*, 1734.

" On Saturday morning, their Majesties and the rest of the royal family went again to Hounslow Heath, where a stag was turned out, which took much the same way as that which was hunted on Wednesday, and was killed near Canons, the seat of his Grace the Duke of Chandos. Their Royal Highnesses the Prince and Duke were in at the death, but their Majesties had quitted the chase some time before."—*Sept.* 1734.

" Yesterday morning, about nine o'clock, their Majesties and the rest of the royal family went from Kensington to Hounslow Heath, where a stag was turned out at the starting-post, which ran directly to Staines ; but being turned, came back as far as Brentford, where he crossed the Thames, and re-crossing at Hampton Town, ran through Staines, and there again crossed the water twice, and was killed about half-an-hour after three, at Water Oakley, near Windsor. Their Majesties gave out at Thorp, about a mile from Staines, after following him about thirty miles ; but their Royal Highnesses the Prince and Duke were in at the death.—*Sept.* 1734.

HOUNSLOW CHURCH.

IT is difficult to rightly determine the etymology of Hounslow. In ancient records it is written Honeslawe, Hundeslaw, and Hunslow, and as it, with the adjacent country, was part of the Warren, or Forest of Staines, which extended from the rivers Colne to Brent, it is highly probable that at this place was an establishment for keeping the hounds that hunted in the forest. *Hundes* in the Saxon language signifying hounds, thence the spot was called Hundeslow, the hounds place, or Hundeslea, the hounds plain, which in process of time was corrupted into Hounslow. We may add that Honeslaw was one of the Six Hundreds of Middlesex enumerated in Domesday Book.

At an early period an hospital was founded here for Friars of the Order of the Holy Trinity. Their peculiar office being to solicit alms to be employed in the ransom of Christians taken captive by the Infi-

dels.* The term by which they were best known was
that of the Trinitarian Brothers of Redemption, while
in France they were generally termed *Mathurins*, after
the name of their founder, Jean Matha, a native of
Provence. Soon after the order was instituted, a
house of it was set up in England, for I find that the
Ministers and Brethren of the Hospital of Hündeslaw
had letters of protection granted to them by King
John. The hospital shared the fate of other Roman
Catholic establishments at the Reformation, and it
being a lesser monastery, whose revenues were under
two hundred pounds per annum, it was by Act of Parliament surrendered to the king.

I need not trouble myself, here, with the history of
this hospital previous to the Reformation, but I may
just relate an anecdote connected with a curious his-
torical fact, very illustrative of the ancient manners
and customs.

Clement Maydestone, a friar of this House, wrote a
history of the martyrdom of Richard Scrope, Archbishop of York, to whom he had been a retainer.

* The custom of taking and retaining in captivity Christians,
by the Infidel states of Northern Africa, was carried on to a
much later period than is generally supposed. In *Applebee's
Journal* of the 9th December, 1721, we read that
"The English captives, who have been redeemed by the late
treaty made with the King of Fez, to the number of two hundred
and eighty persons, marched in their Moorish habits and in good
order, through a great part of the city to the cathedral of St.
Paul's, to return thanks to Almighty God for their redemption
from captivity."

Though there was somewhat of sharp practice used
against the bishop, by inducing him to disband his
army, a story which Shakespeare tells very well, he
was really decollated for treason, and there was no
question of martyrdom about the business. But the
manner of the introduction to Maydestone's story of
the burial of Henry IV. may be quoted here, as it is
illustrative of the custom of receiving the wayfarer to
the hospitalities of the friars' board, and the story was
long believed to be perfectly true.

"After the death of this king, a wonderful event
occurred declaratory of the glory of the above named
Lord Archbishop Richard, and commending it to
memory for ever. For in less than thirty days after
the death of Henry IV., there came a certain man of
his household to the House of the Holy Trinity at
Hundeslaw for refreshment. And while they were
conversing at dinner about the righteousness of that
king's manners, the man said to a certain esquire
named Thomas Maydestone, who was sitting with
him at the table : ' God knows whether he was a good
man ; but this I know for certain, that while his body
was being conveyed in a small vessel from West-
minster towards Canterbury to be buried there, I was
one of three men, who threw the corpse into the river
between Barking and Gravesend.'

" 'And,' he added with an oath, 'such a storm of
wind fell upon us, and the waves run so high, that
many nobles, who followed us in eight small ships,

were scarcely saved from death, their fleet of vessels having been dispersed by the storm. But we, who were with the body, being in peril of our lives, by common consent threw it into the river, and immediately there fell a great calm. But the chest, covered with cloth of gold, in which the body had lain, we carried with great honour into Canterbury, and buried it. Therefore the monks of Canterbury may say, that the sepulchre of King Henry IV. is with us, not his body; as also said Peter of the holy David, in the second chapter of the Acts of the Apostles.' God Almighty is witness and judge that I, Clement Maydestone, saw that man, and heard him swear to my father, Thomas Maydestone, that all that he said was true."

The manuscript, written in Latin, from which the above quotation has been translated, is entitled *Historia Martyrii Ricardi Scrope Archiepiscopi Eboracensis,* and is preserved in the library of Corpus Christi College, Cambridge. But the part I have here quoted was printed by Peck in his *Desiderata Curiosa,* under the title of *Testimonium Clemenetis Maydestone quod Regis Henrici IV., corpus fuit in Thamesin projectum et non tumulatim Cantuariæ.*

The whole manuscript was subsequently printed by Wharton in his *Anglia Sacra,* and it was long a desideratum among antiquaries to test the truth of the story, by an actual examination of the coffin. The royal tomb was accordingly opened in August, 1832,

in the presence of the Lord Bishop of Oxford, the
Dean of Canterbury, and others, and the remains of
the king was found in his coffin. This disposed at
once of the truth of the story told by Maydestone;
and an account of the examination of the tomb,
written by the Rev. Dr. Spry, will be found in the
twenty-sixth volume of the *Archæologia*. And, in
fact, Maydestone may be called an interested witness,
as ready to depreciate the character of the king, as he
was to extol the honour of his master, whom he was
convinced was wrongly executed. And a man whose
prejudices would represent a punishment for high
treason as a martyrdom, and the king's body being
thrown into the Thames as a judgment from Heaven,
would not hesitate to publish the story, far and wide,
even if he did not really invent it, as a proof of divine
interposition, in honour of his patron's memory.

At the Reformation, the Manor of Hounslow and
the site of the Hospital having been annexed by
Henry VIII. to the Honour of Hampton Court, were
leased in 1539 to Richard Awnsham, Esq, for twenty-
one years; and by Edward VI., in 1553, to William
Parr, Marquis of Northampton, for the same term,
commencing after the expiration of Awnsham's lease.
In 1557, the reversion of the said premises, consisting
of the Friars House, one hundred and seventeen acres
of land, with appurtenances, together with the fair,
market, court-leet, &c., was sold for the sum of
£905 13s. 4d., to William, Lord Windsor, whose son,

Edward, Lord Windsor, in 1571, sold the hospital and all its appurtenances, with the demesne lands, to Anthony Roan, Esq., the Queen's Auditor, for the sum of £300, reserving to himself the manor, with the right of holding courts in the great hall of the manor house, and an annual rent of £17, Mr. Roan also binding himself to keep in good repair the tombs of the Windsor family buried in the chapel of the ancient hospital or Friars House.

The Windsors, who lived at Stanwell, buried at Hounslow long before they purchased the manor with the chapel. For Andrews, Lord Windsor, by his will, dated March 26th, 1543, writing himself Andrews Windsor, of Stanwell, Knight, Lord Windsor,* orders his body to be buried :—

"In the choir of the church of the Holy Trinity of Hounslow, in the said county of Middlesex, whether he deceases within the said realm of England or without, if by any reasonable means he could be conveyed thither, and to be placed between the pillars where his entire well-beloved wife, Elizabeth, Lady Windsore, lieth buried ; and that there be made a convenient tomb of free stone, with such arms, images, and scriptures, as shall be thought best by the discretion of his executors ; likewise that his son George's tomb be also finished. That his said burial may be done according to his degree, with such clothing to his household servants, and such mourners as shall be appointed by his executors, and to none others. And that, at the day of his interment, there be twenty-four torches and four great tapers about his hearse, to be holden by twenty-eight poor men, every

---

* He sat in the House of Lords as Baron Windsor, of Bradenham, in Buckinghamshire.

torch weighing sixteen pounds, and every taper containing twelve pounds, every of the poor men, which must belong to the parish of Stanwell, to have sixpence and a gown of frieze."

When Lysons wrote in 1795, there were no vestiges remaining of a tomb to any of the Windsor family, but on the outside of the chapel, towards the road, there was an escutcheon with their arms—a saltier between twelve crosslets. This escutcheon is now placed on the south wall of Hounslow Church. Weever, however, in 1630, took this fragment of an inscription, which is preserved in his *Funeral Monuments.*

"Orate pro animabus Georgii Windsore, filii Andrii Windsore de Stanwell, militis, et Ursule uxoris ejus. . . . "

I may say here that Weever also notices a tomb at Hounslow to one William Jacob, who gave a close, called Bushiheme, to buy a lamp for the chapel. The inscription is as follows, and the Leonine verses which terminate it are very curious examples of their kind :—

"Orate pro anima Willelmi Jacob qui dedit unam clausarum vocatam Bushiheme ad inveniandam unam lampadem . . . qui ob . . . 1478.
"Vermibus hic donor, et sic ostendere conor,
Qualiter hic ponor, ponitur omnis honor.
Quisquis ades tu morte cades ota respice plora
Sum quod eris, quod es ipse fui pro me precor ora."

Could Bushiheme, from this very circumstance, have subsequently taken the name of Lampton, which belongs to a district in the neighbourhood at the present day ?

But to return to Queen Elizabeth's auditor, Anthony Roan, we find by a pedigree in the Harleian Manuscripts, that he was living at Hounslow towards the close of her reign. The manor of Hounslow and its appurtenances then went through a long series of the vicissitudes that ever attend landed property, till at last, in the year 1705, it was bought by Whitelock Bulstrode, Esq. From him, who died in 1724, it descended to his grandson, Richard Bulstrode, Esq., whose widow became the lady of the manor. At her death it went to Gardner Bulstrode, a distant relation and a bachelor. This gentleman, who died in 1822, bequeathed it in trust to be sold, the proceeds to be laid out in stock, the dividends to be paid to his sister Elizabeth during her natural life, and afterwards in trust to pay certain legacies amounting to between nine and ten thousand pounds, (including £1000 to the British and Foreign Bible Society, and a like sum to the Worcester Infirmary), and the residue to the five daughters of Mrs. Catherine Newsham of Chelsea, daughter of the said Elizabeth, who were all married. When the mansion at Hounslow, as well as the manor with its immunities were sold, Mrs. Newsham's sons-in-law, viz., James Minns, Esq., of Harrow ; James Eades, Esq., of Sevenoaks ; John Willesford, Esq., of Chelsea ; John Nichols, Esq., of the same place ; and George Edwards, Esq., of Birmingham ; purchased the latter as tenants in common, and I believe they still retain it, receiving the tolls at the fair.

All the Bulstrode property, in this neighbourhood, was sold in the year 1818 to Thomas Cane, Esq.

There is not a vestige of the ancient manor house extant, more than the wall in front of it, which runs a short distance up Lampton Lane. Nor do I think that it has ever been engraved, as all my researches to obtain a view of it have been utterly unavailable

When Mr. Lysons wrote in 1795, the only remaining part of the hospital was the chapel, which I have engraved from his *Environs*, as a frontispiece to this little *brochure*. The interior comprised a chancel, nave, and south aisle It exhibited evident traces of the architecture that prevailed in the early part of the thirteenth century, particularly in its stone stalls, three of which were to be seen in the south wall of the chancel, and a double piscina, with narrow pointed arches, divided by a column. This chapel, since the Reformation, has been used as a place of worship for the inhabitants of Hounslow, and the names of the curates or chaplains, as near as they can be made out, with the dates of their appointments, are here given .—

John Pight	1561	Samuel Rowles	1669
Milo Barrow	1580	John Godfrey	1715
Samuel Hill	1592	Law. Brandreth	1718
——— Bradshaw	1612	J. W. Williams	1742
John Gainsforde	1615	W. Fetherstone	1742
Ben. Geering	1637	Wetenhall Wilkes	1748
Henry Walker	1664	John Chapeau	1772
	Joseph Benson	1814.	

The chapel was repaired in 1705, by Whitelock Bulstrode, Esq., soon after his purchase of the manor; and a great part of it was afterwards destroyed by fire, early in the seventeenth century, when it was restored by the assistance of a brief. Probably the restoration took place in 1710, for over the door of the old chapel there was a stone with the inscription—

DOMUS DEI
ORNATA
AN. DOM.
1710.

It is now placed in the vestry of the church. The present church being erected on the site of the ancient chapel, the greatest care was taken of the sacred relics of the dead, and any inscription, any sculptured stone pertaining thereto, was with the greatest of good feeling and good taste, built up in the new building. I may only mention, however, the monument of Whitelocke Bulstrode, which was attached to the north wall of the chancel, and is now placed at the east end of the north gallery in the present chapel; it has the following inscription—

In hâc suâ capellâ, in conditorio prope hoc marmor per seipsum structo, reliquias suas jacere voluit Whitelocke Bulstrode, Arm. Sacræ theologiæ amator, philosophiæ naturalis

cultor, justitiæ moderator ; animi caritate, morum probitate
clarus, in suos amantissimus, in totum genus humanum benignus.
Filius fuit Richardi Bulstrode, Militis, ad Bruxellas a regibus
Carolo Secundo et Jacobo Secundo plurimis annis legati ; nepos
Edwardi Bulstrode de Soley-end, in Com. Warw. Arm., Walliæ
Septentrionalis Capital. Justic. pronepos Edwardi Bulstrode de
Bulstrode in Com. Bucks. Arm Obiit 27 die Novembris, anno
Dom. 1724, Ætatis 74. M.S. patris benignissimi H.M.S.

The ancient chapel and a small portion of the
adjoining ground was purchased from the above-
mentioned Mr. Cane, by the Rev. H. S Trimmer,
vicar of Heston, who generously presented it to the
Church Society. And his Majesty's commissioners,
under the act for building churches and chapels,
agreed that if the neighbourhood would raise £2000,
towards defraying the expense of building a new
chapel, they would advance the remainder. Pope tells
us that he

"Who builds a church to God, and not to fame,
Will never mark the marble with his name ;"

so I am induced here to give the original names of the
subscribers to Hounslow Chapel, from the old sub-
scription list.

	£	s.		£	s.
Duke of Northumberland	500	0	Rev. J. Benson, D.D.	255	0
Howley, Bishop of Lon-			Rev. H. Glossop, vicar		
don	105	0	of Isleworth . . .	200	0
Rev. H. S. Trimmer .	303*	0	S. Adams, Esq. . .	10	0

* This was not paid in money, but the ground and old materials of the ancient chapel were considered as an equivalent.

	£	s.		£	s.
Andrews, Esq. . . .	5	0	Mr. Gotelee	5	0
Miss Andrews . . .	2	0	Mr. Gotelee, Jun. . .	1	0
Jas. Aslett, Esq. . .	10	0	Mr. Gough	1	0
Lady Banks	50	0	Mr. Gray	2	0
Rev. J. S. Baron . .	2	2	Mr. J. W. Greenfield .	1	1
Mr. Beckley	2	0	Mrs. Hesketh . . .	70	0
J. Bentall, Esq. . . .	5	0	Mr. Hiscock	2	0
Miss Bickham . . .	5	0	R. Hope, Esq. . . .	5	0
Mr. Body	3	0	R. How, Esq. . . .	100	0
Mr. Boughton . . .	5	0	Mr. Jennings . . .	5	0
Mr. Bristow	10	0	Mr. Lambourn . . .	0	10
Mr. W. Butler . . .	10	0	W. Langdon, Esq. .	100	0
Miss Butler	5	0	Mr. Ledger	1	0
G. Channer, Esq. . .	10	0	Mr. Lidgold	10	0
Mr. Charlton. . . .	5	5	Rev. J. Morgan . . .	5	0
Col. Clitherow . . .	50	0	T. Palmer, Esq. . .	50	0
W. Cole, Esq. . . .	10	0	Rev. W. H. Parker .	10	0
Mr. Coomes	3	0	Mrs. Persley . . .	3	0
Mr. Davis	5	0	H. Pownall, Esq. . .	30	0
W. Day, Esq. . . .	25	0	Mrs. H. Pownall . .	20	0
John Dixon, Esq. . .	20	0	Mr. Sambrook . . .	1	0
J. Ede, Esq.	10	0	Mr. Slark.	5	0
Mr. Eley	1	1	J. W. Smith, Esq. . .	20	0
H. Farnell, Esq. . .	25	0	Messrs. Stanbrough . .	20	0
Messrs. J. & C. Farnell	100	0	J. Stanbrough, Esq. .	30	0
Mr. Filley	5	0	Mrs. Strange. . . .	1	0
Mr. Franks	30	0	Mr. Such	2	0
R. A. Frogley, Esq. .	20	0	Mr. P. Walker . . .	10	0
Mrs. Fish	50	0	Mrs. Walker. . . .	5	0
Mrs. Gay	2	0	Mrs. Westbrook . .	20	0
Mr. George	1	0	Messrs. White	20	0
Mr. Goddard. . . .	5	0	H. Wilkinson, Esq. .	20	0
Mr. Goodchild . . .	1	0	J. Wilmot, Esq. . . .	10	0
Mrs. Gostling . . .	50	0			

The old chapel was pulled down, its materials were

sold, and the foundation stone of the present church was laid by the Duke of Northumberland, in June, 1828; and it was completed and opened for divine service in July, 1829. In 1836 it was thought expedient by his Majesty's Commissioners, to consolidate the adjoining parts of the parishes of Heston and Isleworth into a distinct district, to be assigned to this church for all ecclesiastical purposes, under the name of the consolidated chapelry of Hounslow. The Bishop of London, as rector of Heston, has the patronage of this living, only two clergyman have been appointed to the church since it was built. The Rev. Joseph Benson, D.D.,* who had for fourteen years been the clergyman of the old chapel ; and after him, the Rev. Edward East, M.A., our present worthy incumbent.

* In my collection of prints there is an engraved portrait of the Rev. J. Benson, D.D., of Hounslow, fol. size, published in 1851.

HOUNSLOW HEATH.

THE Heath has a great history, peculiarly its own, as a place for mustering and encamping the large armies formerly raised in England. Its contiguity to London, and its being on the way to Staines Bridge,* then the only bridge on the river, besides London Bridge, and the direct road to Portsmouth, then the usual place of embarkation, made it peculiarly eligible for mustering the armies employed by the kings of England to enforce their claims to the throne of

---

* Three oak trees were granted by the Crown, out of Windsor Forest, in 1262, for the repair of Staines Bridge; and I may observe here that the first gunpowder manufactured in England, was most probably on Hounslow Heath; for a William of Staines was employed by Edward the Third, in 1346, to make the gunpowder which helped to gain the memorable battle of Cressy, the very first time that English cannon were used in war.

France. Here also, in 1267, the Earl of Gloucester mustered his rebellious Londoners, and threatened to give battle to Henry III., but found it expedient to withdraw before the arrival of the royal forces. Later still the army of Henry VII., marching to London, victors from the Field of Bosworth, and carrying with them the deadly pestilence of the sweating sickness, encamped on the Heath. In the Great Rebellion it was found very useful for a similar purpose. Charles the First, after the disastrous battle of Brentford, in 1642, entrenched his troops there. In the very same year it was occupied by the Parliamentary army, commanded by the Earl of Essex. In 1647, the Parliamentary forces under Sir Thomas Fairfax, were assembled on the Heath, to the number of 20,000 horse and foot, with a suitable train of artillery. A grand review took place here of the whole army, which was drawn up in battalions to the length of nearly a mile and a half, and the Speakers of both Houses of Parliament, together with most of the members, accompanied the general in a progress from regiment to regiment through the army, and were received with great acclamations. It was on the Heath, too, that James the Second raised his army, in the vain attempt to prostrate the liberties and religion of Englishmen. In the library of the Corporation of London, at Guildhall, there are three different Views of James the Second's Camp on Hounslow Heath

One is entitled—*An Exact Prospect of the King's*

Forces encamped on Hounslow Heath, 1686. It is a wood-cut.

Another is, the *Camp on Hounslow Heath,* 1686. It is also a wood-cut, but has a letter-press description.

The third is, *The Prospect of the Royal Army encamped on Hounslow Heath.* This is a copper-plate, engraved by Harris.

In the first volume of *Poems on Affairs of State,* there is sometimes found a very rare second part, with a different pagination, entitled *State Poems continued,* in which there is one extremely severe on James, called *Hounslow Heath,* 1686. It is also severe on the poet Dryden, calling him—

"Old Squab, the hungry bard that writes for pension."

Mr. Wilkes seems not to have had an antiquarian turn of mind, for he does not allude to any of these camps in his poem; not even to a camp that was formed on the Heath, in 1740, just a few years before he wrote. This camp was formed in June, under the command of Sir Charles Wills, and I may add a few jottings of it here from newspaper cuttings in my possession.

"*List of the General Officers and Forces under encampment.*

"Camp at Hounslow.—Sir Charles Wills, General; Lord Mark Ker, Lieutenant-General; — Cornwall,

Major-General ; — Folliot, and the Earl of Albemarle, Brigadiers.

"Forces ordered to encamp under the command of
Sir Charles Wills, on Hounslow Heath, are two troops
of Horse Guards, one troop of Horse Grenadiers, and
three regiments of foot consisting of seven battalions."
—*May 29th,* 1740.

"It having been represented to his Majesty, that
the troops that encamp on Hounslow Heath will not
be able to support themselves with their present pay,
orders are given that an allowance of a pound and a
half of bread per day be delivered to each private
sentinel, for which they are to pay no more than five
farthings."—*June 7th,* 1740.

"The encampment on Hounslow Heath will cer-
tainly take place to-morrow, to the great joy of all
the towns and villages in the neighbourhood, which
have for some days been so crowded with soldiers,
both horse and foot, that some inns have had four or
five and twenty quartered upon them at once.

"We are assured that the prevailing reason for this
camp is to instruct the new-raised men, and the young
officers, in the nature of encampments, and not from
any apprehensions of an invasion, as has been pre-
tended.

"The Right Hon. the Earl of Albemarle has hired
the Warrener's house on Hounslow Heath, being near

where his lordship's troop encamps, to reside in during the encampment."—*June* 15*th*, 1740.

"Yesterday morning, the second troop of Horse Guards, commanded by his Grace the Duke of Marlborough, and the third troop commanded by the Earl of Albemarle; the first troop of Horse Grenadier Guards, commanded by General Dormer; the first regiment of Foot Guards, commanded by General Wills; the second commanded by his Royal Highness the Duke of Cumberland; and the third, commanded by the Earl of Dunmore; were reviewed in Hyde Park, by Sir Charles Wills, after which they marched for their encampment on Hounslow Heath." —*June* 19*th*, 1740.

" The baggage and furniture belonging to his Royal Highness the Duke of Cumberland, was carried from St. James's to Hounslow, and last night his Royal Highness went thither and lay in his tent, where he designs to continue during the encampment there."

I learn from another newspaper paragraph, that the tent was a magnificent one, containing several apartments, and cost one hundred pounds.

"Yesterday his Royal Highness the Duke gave a grand entertainment to the officers encamped on Hounslow Heath; great quantities of wine and provision having been sent on Sunday night, from St. James's for that purpose.

"We hear that his Royal Highness the Duke of

Cumberland, the Duke of Marlborough, the Earl of Albemarle, and Sir Charles Wills, intend to keep open tables in their tents during the encampment on Hounslow Heath.

"Yesterday a train of artillery was carried through the city for the camp at Hounslow."—*June 24th,* 1740.

The Royal Duke does not appear to have stopped long at the camp, for I read, that—

"Yesterday morning, the plate, &c., belonging to his Royal Highness the Duke of Cumberland, was brought from his tent at Hounslow to St. James's, and the same evening his baggage, plate, &c, was carried from thence, under a strong guard, to Portsmouth, his Highness being to set out on Saturday next for that place, in order to go as a volunteer on board the Victory, a first-rate, under the command of Sir John Norris."—*July 3rd,* 1740.

It is, perhaps, too much the custom now to speak slightingly of the Duke of Cumberland, for the severities he exercised upon the Highlanders after the battle of Culloden; but his policy was really merciful, as it effectually prevented another rebellion, in favour of the Stuarts. The Duke, being the first prince of the Brunswick family who was born in England, piqued himself through life upon being an Englishman. Riding out one morning to a review with his father, George II., when he was not above ten years of age, two officers, who admired the look of the young hero, could not resist exclaiming, " What a charming boy that is !" The young duke overheard them, and thinking they said *German* instead of *charming*, turned round in a great heat and exclaimed, " 'Tis false, gentlemen ; I am am no German, I'm an English boy, and I beg you may never call me so again."

" On Sunday night last two soldiers of the Second Regiment of Foot Guards strayed out of the camp at Hounslow into a farmer's ground adjacent, with a design to make free with some of his sheep, but the farmer's servant seeing them, shot one of them through the back that he instantly died, and wounded the other, so that his life is despaired of."—*July 1st,* 1740.

" The soldier that was shot by a farmer's servant near Hounslow in a sheep robbery, and committed by Justice Clitheroe to Newgate for the same, is much amended since his commitment, and is in a fair way to the gallows."—*July 5th,* 1740.

" On Sunday there was, as it is thought, above twenty thousand people to visit the camp at Hounslow, insomuch that it was a very difficult task for the soldiers that stood sentinel to keep the mob from breaking in upon the lines, and such crowds flocked down by water, that at one view might be seen two hundred boats on the river making for Isleworth stairs."

July 8th, 1740.

The " silent highway" was maintained as a channel of transport for both passengers and goods all along the valley of the Thames to a very late period. The watermen's fares from London to Windsor, and the intermediate places, was published so late as 1828. All the market garden produce then came to London by boat to Hungerford Market, and the peculiar boat used is engraved in Pyne's *Microcosm*, where it is styled the "Battersea Gardener's Boat." From Griffith's *Essay on the Jurisdiction of the Thames*, we learn that the fare from London to Isleworth in 1746 was three and sixpence for a wherry that could contain eight passengers. If the passengers, however, numbered eight and elected to go by company, as it was termed, their fare was only sixpence each. We learn, also, that the Windsor carriers then sailed twice a week from Queenhithe. In a *Voyage up the Thames*, published in 1738, there is an account of a public-house at Isleworth kept open all night, as a sort of night house, for the express accommodation of parties travelling by the Thames, " so that they should not fail of entertainment any hour of the night." The writer tells us that—

" In the rooms for the reception of all visitors, into which we were conducted, we found some hardship to get seats, and more to come near the fire; but the mixed appearance of the company promised some diversion in recompense for that disappointment."

"From the camp at Hounslow we hear that the

suttlers make a fine account of it there, by the great concourse of people that are continually flocking to see the novelty, though they have been put under a military contribution, if it may so be said ; and some of them, it is said, have been at above one hundred pounds expense for the liberty of suttling there."

"Provisions of all sorts are at a high price in the camp at Hounslow, which being at present a novelty, the country come in on all sides, and prodigious crowds of people are every day upon the heath, from town as well as from adjacent parts. This encampment is likely to prove very expensive to the officers in entertainments, unless their friends will think proper to have some mercy on them, and be sparing of their visits."

I may close my jottings of this camp with a tragical one, as follows :—

"On Monday last died at Wimbledon, after a few days' illness, occasioned by a fright she took from the horses running away with her, when she was with her husband in a chaise at the camp at Hounslow, Mrs. Wills, wife to Captain Wills, nephew to the Right Honourable Sir Charles Wills, Knight of the Bath, and on Friday night her corpse is to be interred at Stanmore. Mrs. Wills was far gone with child when this unfortunate accident happened."

This camp at Hounslow Heath created such an interest in the minds of the public that it was painted, and the picture became a popular exhibition ; this we learn from the following advertisement which appeared in the Daily Advertiser of March 13th, 1744 :—

"To be seen, at One Shilling each Person, at the Swan, at the bottom of Hay Hill, Dover Street.

"The Whole Prospect of the late CAMP at HOUNS-LOW HEATH, representing, in proper Order, both Horse and Foot, every Officer in his proper Post, with the nicest distinction of both their Liveries and Colours; in Proportion and Magnitude, representing Life nearer than anything of that kind hitherto invented. The Train of Artillery in its proper Decorum.

"Note.—And it has been seen only by their Royal Highnesses the Prince and Princess of Wales.

"To be seen from Nine in the Morning till Six in the Evening."

THE END.

J. C. Hotten, 74 &' 75, *Piccadilly.*

Lightning Source UK Ltd.
Milton Keynes UK
UKHW020640140621
385483UK00005B/381